MW00462134

# french omelettes

m

# french omelettes

## YOUR NEW HOUSE MEAL

written & photographed by

## marc j. sievers

**LITTLE PRINCE PRESS**

CHICAGO

m

Marc J. Sievers is also the author of:

> *Entertaining with Love*—Inspired Recipes for Everyday Entertaining
> *Table for Two*—Cooking and Entertaining for You and Your +1

Visit Marc's website: MarcSievers.com

Sievers, Marc J.
French Omelettes: Your new house meal / Marc J. Sievers
Includes recipe index.
Cooking; Recipes

Library of Congress Cataloging-in-Publication Data is on file with the publisher.

ISBN-13: 978-1-7332885-0-7

LITTLE PRINCE
PRESS

Published in the United States by Little Prince Press, an imprint of Marc-Ryan Group
Chicago Illinois USA 60611
Visit our website: marc-ryan.com/lpp
American made. Printed in the United States of America | 1

m

*I dedicate this book to home cooks everywhere. Whether
you grew up in the kitchen, like me, or found your own
path to cooking, I encourage you to keep learning,
celebrating, and having an adventure in your kitchen.
Eat well, laugh often, and share the love!*

Marc
xo

# Introduction

*"The difference between a good cook and a great cook is confidence and the best ingredients.  The rest is debatable!"*

—Marc J. Sievers

# FRENCH OMELETTES

———— m ————

I have been wanting to write a book dedicated to French omelettes for a long time. My love affair with this classic bistro staple began when I was ten-ish years old and first saw a re-run of *The Omelette Show* episode of Julia Child's *The French Chef* on PBS while snuggling on the sofa with my nan. It was truly a landmark moment in which Julia made lots (and lots!) of omelettes for a dinner party, serving them with a variety of toppings and using ingredients I recognized from cooking in the kitchen with nan. I was just a child then and it was the first time I learned what a French omelette was. I thought it was all so sophisticated and chic (I came out only a few years later!). Near the end of that episode, Julia walks from her set kitchen into her set dining room (with decorative chickens on the table and sideboard—*that* explains why I collect chickens!) to close the show—and it is that moment I think of each and every time I make an omelette.

More about nan (who actually never made us omelettes)—she was *the* It Girl in our family. Nan cared for all of us, cooked for all of us, made us laugh, and loved us all harder than anyone could ever explain. I grew up with strong women in my life and everyone looked out for one another—nothing has changed. We didn't have a lot growing up and even lived in a government housing community. But those were the days of pure happiness and bliss, and somehow there was always a home-cooked meal on the table. We all loved being in the kitchen together—nothing has changed there, either. The stories of nan and my aunties all playing cards at the kitchen table, drinking cheap Boone's Farm wine, and smoking cigarettes (with nan continuously lighting the filter end) are stories that are told each and every time we are all together. That is what the kitchen and cooking does for us—they help create lasting memories that are still laugh-your-ass-off worthy decades later.

Right, this book is about omelettes! Do these magical omelettes deserve an entire book? Yes! Because even as a little boy I was fascinated by how quickly Julia's omelettes came together and the technique involved in making them—jerking the pan just so, folding the sides of the cooked egg onto itself, then gently plating it for serving. I loved that it didn't need to be absolutely perfect. Even Julia would fix her own omelettes a bit with a fork if it didn't fold just right onto the plate, and rubbed more

———— ccc ————

butter on it to give it a shine. And, I loved the end of each episode of her show when Julia would also show us how to set a the table and how to entertain with the meal that she just made. She reminded me of my nan—a sturdy lady with a unique charm and a giving soul. See, I told you omelettes were magical!

French omelettes are more than just a breakfast food. They are a main course to be served at any time of the day or night for an especially chic but earthy way to entertain. Dinner parties do not have to be about preparing course after course, getting up and down every ten minutes and driving yourself crazy making sure things are perfect. I would much rather sit with you and have my leg fall asleep, eat too much cheese, and lose count of the opened bottles of wine! Pair a French omelette with a couple of sides and a delicious dessert, and you have a memorable meal that you will love serving to your guests, and that they will love to eat. Great wine, candles, and grocery store flowers are the only other accessories you need—well, that and courage in the kitchen. It really is that simple.

French omelettes have become my house meal—my one go-to meal that I feel confident serving to my guests, regardless of the time of day. I serve them to everyone who visits for the first time and many times thereafter, and I have for almost two decades. In this book I wanted to share my love for French omelettes and explore how amazingly versatile (and easy!) they are. They take less time to make than pancakes in the morning; they fit the bill for a Parisian-style brunch with a tartine and a glass of wine; they are the quintessential dinner party "trick up your sleeve"; as well as a quick snack for an after-dark kitchen rendezvous to end an evening spent out on the town! Remember the late-night kitchen scene with Diane Keaton and Jack Nicholson from the movie *Something's Gotta Give*—attempting to make pancakes but getting interrupted? A French omelette would have helped to seal the deal faster.

We have become accustomed to seeking out recipes that will take as little time in the kitchen as possible to get meals on the table around the clock. Work, family, and life definitely make time of the essence, but I do think it is important to confidently learn your way around your kitchen and master basic cooking techniques. A few basics are all you need for this entire book. When I first decided to learn how to make my

own French omelettes I bought a couple dozen eggs, got a good nonstick pan, loaded my 6-disc CD player with my favorite tunes, grabbed some butter, and got to work. Many under-cooked, overly-browned, and misshapen omelettes later and I was making my own beautifully folded French omelettes. You can do it, too. It takes patience, a few flicks of the wrist, and practice (set your phone to 'do not disturb': this will require your full attention). Once you have mastered my simplified technique of making a plain French omelette, it will only take about 30 seconds from pan to plate, making it the ultimate fast food. What other meal can you pull together in less than a minute?

After the plain omelette has been mastered, the fun really begins! For this book I have created 30 omelette recipes, each vegetable-focused, that add beautiful and savory layers of flavor, from simple to more complex, perfectly tailored for any occasion. There are also 13 vegetarian recipes for components that can be served alongside any of the omelettes featured in the book, or with any dishes you already have in your own repertoire. In addition to the gorgeous colorful vegetables, fresh herbs are everywhere on these pages! They add texture, flavor, and a freshness that elevates even the unassuming egg to new heights. Herbs truly showcase how a few simple ingredients can be transformed into a company-worthy meal, any time of day! With only a few exceptions all of the ingredients featured in my recipes can be found at your local grocery store. Any harder-to-find ingredients are noted on page 25 and can be bought online or at specialty grocers (and I mean that—there are only a few). If you are really in a pinch, even your neighborhood convenience store is sure to have eggs, butter, salt, and pepper!

I researched and recipe tested *French Omelettes* in Paris; one of my favorite cities in the world, and the best place to dive deeply into how this wonderfully easy and iconic dish became a mainstay in French cuisine and culture. This book is the culmination of a lifetime of inspiration begun by *The Omelette Show* episode, and my nan and her love of teaching me to cook. I am thrilled to be able to share my inspiration with home cooks everywhere. The classic French omelette is earthy and elegant, and is the perfect example of how simplicity always wins. I am confident that you will also become a French omelette expert and I hope that you will make it your house meal, too. Now, let's get started!

# Ingredients Index

These five basic ingredients are found in most recipes throughout this cookbook:

Black Pepper

Eggs

Fleur de Sel

Sea Salt

Unsalted Butter

**A**

Artichoke Hearts (frozen) – 111

Arugula – 55, 59, 71, 85

Asparagus – 59, 67

Avocado – 49, 75

**B**

Baguette – 63, 69, 85

Balsamic Vinegar – 79

Basil – 31, 35, 45, 47, 49, 59, 73, 75, 79, 109, 113

Bread (country / boule) – 31

Brioche – 103

Broccoli – 49

Burrata – 35, 42

**C**

Camembert Cheese – 43, 123

Carrots – 29, 117

Cayenne Pepper – 29

Champagne Vinegar – 115

Chèvre Cheese – 43, 123

Chili Powder – 29

Chives – 31, 39, 59, 61, 77, 109, 113, 117

Chocolate (dark) – 121

Cinnamon – 121

Cocoa Powder – 121

Cognac – 121

Comté Cheese – 43, 123

Cranberry Juice – 125

Crème Fraîche – 43, 51, 69, 109, 115, 117, 121

**D**

Dijon Mustard – 33, 103, 115, 117

Dill – 39, 41, 59, 61, 109, 113

**E**

Eggplant (graffiti) – 53, 119

Elderflower Liqueur – 125

Endive – 77

English Cheddar – 43, 47

**F**

Fennel – 53, 65

Fontina Cheese (Val d'Aosta) – 41, 43, 67, 79

French Feta – 43, 55

**G**

Garlic – 31, 35, 37, 53, 59, 67, 77, 101, 105, 109, 115, 119

Garlic (deeply roasted) – 39

# Ingredients Index

# Ingredients Index

# Omelette Recipes

## AROUND-THE-CLOCK ENTERTAINING WITH YOUR NEW HOUSE MEAL

*"My idea of a fabulous Saturday night?  Simple food, great wine, and lots of laughter.  Is there anything better?!"*

—Marc J. Sievers

# Before You Get Started!

## MY TRIED-AND-TRUE FRENCH OMELETTE TIPS

**Small prep bowls**—the process of making my Simple French Omelette (next page) starts and finishes in the blink of an eye, I'm talking 20 – 30 seconds! I always have 4 prep bowls pre-filled with beaten eggs, salt, and pepper. This will keep you and your kitchen counter organized and will make the process of quickly cooking each individual omelette base less intimidating from the get-go. The recipes here are measured to make 4 plated omelettes but can easily be expanded to suit your entertaining needs.

**Eggs**—I use extra-large eggs, as fresh as possible (get to know your local farmer!), and always at room temperature. In fact, I don't refrigerate fresh eggs, especially if I know I will use up a dozen (or two!) over the course of a week. Eggs are hermetically sealed little packages—just make sure to examine each egg to ensure they are free from small cracks.

**Butter**—in order to control the amount of salt in each omelette I use unsalted, room-temperature butter. Also, French or Irish butter will add richer flavor to your omelettes and components. If those butters are unavailable, choose a European-style or organic butter. Just as I do with eggs, I don't refrigerate my butter. I keep mine covered in a glass dish with a tight-fitting lid, away from the heat of the stove and sunlight.

**Omelette pan**—having the perfect pan is the key to making the quintessential French omelette each and every time! I use the Calphalon® Contemporary Nonstick 10-Inch Omelet Pan which can be found in stores that sell quality cookware or online. This pan is sturdy, lightweight, easy to manipulate, and wipes clean with a warm, soapy dishcloth.

**Harder-to-find ingredients**—almost every ingredient in this book can be found at most local grocery stores. There are just a handful of specialty ingredients that are really worth finding and can be ordered online:

Pink Peppercorns

Edible Gold Leaf (*either in the form of small sheets or in a shaker*)

Fleur de Sel (*which is French sea salt—not just coarse sea salt*)

Truffle Salt (*black or white variety*)

White Truffle Butter

Truffle Oil (*black or white variety*)

Summer Black Truffles Carpaccio

*Note: I use Urbani Truffles products, which you can order online at Urbani.com*

# Simple French Omelette

## PRACTICE MAKES PERFECT

### DIRECTIONS

① In a small bowl, beat the eggs, salt, and pepper until the yolks and whites are fully incorporated.

② Place a 10-inch nonstick frying pan over high heat. Allow the pan to get very hot, but not smoking.

③ Add the butter and swirl it around to evenly coat the bottom and sides of the pan. Once the butter is completely melted and the foam has started to subside, pour the eggs into the center of the butter (be careful to not let the butter turn brown).

### INGREDIENTS & PREP

**Eggs** - 2 extra-large, at room temperature, as fresh as possible

**Sea Salt** - ¼ teaspoon

**Black Pepper** - ¼ teaspoon, freshly cracked

**Butter** - 1 tablespoon, unsalted, at room temperature, French recommended

—

*Makes 1 omelette, multiply recipe as needed*

④ Allow the eggs to sit for just 5 – 10 seconds before you begin swirling the pan over the heat, until the edges just start to cook, and the center of the eggs begins to bubble.

⑤ Continue the swirling motion for another 5 – 10 seconds. Once the eggs begin to set and there is just a little bit of wetness in the center, jerk the pan several times back and forth in order to fold the eggs onto itself. The finished omelette will end up in the far lip of the pan.

⑥ Grasp the handle of the pan from underneath and rest the far lip of the pan (where the omelette has formed) slightly off-center onto the bottom of a dinner plate.

⑦ Gently turn the pan upside down over the plate to drop the omelette into position.

**Et voilà**—the perfect French omelette!

# Carrot & Spicy Yogurt Crèma Omelette
## TOASTED PISTACHIOS ADD A NUTTY CRUNCH

## DIRECTIONS

*SPICY YOGURT CRÈMA*

① In a small bowl, add all of the ingredients. Whisk until smooth. Set aside.

*ROASTED CARROTS*

② Preheat the oven to 400 degrees F.

③ Place the carrots onto a half sheet pan. Drizzle over the olive oil, and add the salt and pepper. Toss to coat.

④ Roast for 15 minutes, toss, and continue roasting for another 10 minutes, until the carrots are tender and the edges are lightly browned. During the last 5 minutes in the oven, add the whole shelled pistachios. Remove the sheet pan from the oven and set aside.

⑤ Prepare my *Simple French Omelette* (page 27). As you plate each omelette, spoon over 1 – 2 tablespoons of the yogurt crèma, roasted carrot and pistachios, and scatter over fresh parsley.

**Entertaining Idea:** A big green salad, dressed in my *Everyday Lemon Vinaigrette* (page 103), and a baguette is all you need to accompany this omelette. The carrots become tender and caramelized—it really is a hearty dish! If there are leftover carrots, I like to put them on a slice of thick country bread that has been toasted, shmeared with goat cheese, drizzled with a little honey, and a pinch of red pepper flakes—an instant tartine for a snack!

## INGREDIENTS & PREP

*SPICY YOGURT CRÈMA*

**Greek Yogurt** - ½ cup, full fat, at room temperature

**Mascarpone Cheese** - 3 tablespoons, at room temperature

**Heavy Cream** - ¼ cup, at room temperature

**Cayenne Pepper** - ½ teaspoon

**Chili Powder** - ½ teaspoon

**Smoked Paprika** - ¼ teaspoon, hot variety

**Sea Salt** - ¼ teaspoon

*ROASTED CARROTS*

**Carrots** - 1 pound, peeled, cut diagonally into 1-inch lengths, tri-colored variety

**Olive Oil** - ¼ cup

**Sea Salt** - ¾ teaspoon

**Black Pepper** - ½ teaspoon, freshly cracked

**Pistachios** - ½ cup, whole, shelled, unsalted

**Parsley** - ½ cup, whole leaves, fresh, Italian flat-leaf variety

—

*Serves 4*

# Tartine *á l'*Omelette

TOASTED COUNTRY BREAD MAKES THE PERFECT CRISPY BASE

## DIRECTIONS

*TARTINE BASE*

① Preheat the oven to 400 degrees F. Line a half sheet pan with parchment paper.

② Brush one side of each slice of bread with olive oil and place olive-side up onto the prepared pan. Bake for 8 – 10 minutes, until the bread is crisp and golden brown.

③ Remove the pan from the oven and rub each oiled side of the bread with the garlic clove. Top each slice with Gruyère cheese, return to the oven and bake for another 1 – 2 minutes, until the cheese is melted. Remove the pan from the oven and set aside.

*CREAMY WILTED SPINACH*

④ While the bread is baking, in a medium sauté pan set over medium heat, add the vinaigrette and olive oil. Once hot, add the baby spinach and cook for 3 – 5 minutes, stirring occasionally, until wilted. Set aside.

⑤ Transfer the toasted bread slices to large dinner plates. Evenly spoon over the hot spinach mixture onto the bread.

⑥ Prepare my *Simple French Omelette* (page 27). Plate each omelette on top of the wilted spinach mixture and sprinkle over Parmesan shavings. Garnish with basil, chives and microgreens.

## INGREDIENTS & PREP

*TARTINE BASE*

**Country Bread** – 4 slices, about 10-inches long each, good crusty bakery boule

**Olive Oil** – 4 tablespoons

**Garlic** – 1 clove

**Gruyère Cheese** – 2 cups, freshly grated, divided

*CREAMY WILTED SPINACH*

**French Bistro Vinaigrette** – 1 cup, page 115

**Olive Oil** – 3 tablespoons

**Baby Spinach** – 6 ounces

**Parmesan Cheese** – 1 cup, large shavings, Parmigiano-Reggiano recommended

**Basil** – ½ cup, whole leaves, fresh

**Chives** – ½ cup, fresh, cut into 1-inch lengths

**Microgreens** – ½ cup

—

*Serves 4*

**Tip**: The key to plating this omelette is timing. You want the Gruyère-topped bread to just come out of the oven when you top it with the creamy wilted spinach mixture. That way there are only a few minutes in between while you make and plate the omelettes. None of the steps are difficult, they just take some kitchen coordination—et voilà!

# Citrus Olive Tapenade Omelette

## AN ODE TO A PROVENÇAL KITCHEN

### DIRECTIONS

1. In a medium bowl, add all of the ingredients. Using a fork or hand-held pastry blender, gently blend the mixture to have a coarse texture.

2. Prepare my *Simple French Omelette* (page 27). As you plate each omelette, divide the tapenade evenly over each omelette. Garnish with more parsley.

**Tip:** You can make this up to 2 days in advance. Store it in an airtight container in the refrigerator. I like to add a little more fresh parsley, salt, and pepper before serving.

**Entertaining Idea:** You can also serve this as an hors d'oeuvre on toasted baguette slices or crackers.

### INGREDIENTS & PREP

**Black Olives** - 6 ounces, pitted, drained

**Sun-Dried Tomatoes** - 1½ tablespoons, roughly chopped, packed in oil variety

**Parmesan Cheese** - 2 tablespoons, freshly grated, Parmigiano-Reggiano recommended

**Dijon Mustard** - 1 teaspoon

**Thyme** - 1 teaspoon, minced, fresh

**Parsley** - 1 tablespoon, roughly chopped, fresh, Italian flat-leaf variety, plus more for garnish

**Lemon Zest** - ½ teaspoon, freshly zested

**Sea Salt** - ¼ teaspoon

**Black Pepper** - ¼ teaspoon, freshly cracked

—

*Serves 4*

### NOTES

# Caprese Omelette

SHERRY VINEGAR LIVENS UP EVEN OUT-OF-SEASON TOMATOES

## DIRECTIONS

① In a medium bowl, add all of the ingredients, reserving the burrata and basil, and gently stir to combine. Allow the tomatoes to sit at room temperature for 30 minutes.

② Prepare my *Simple French Omelettes* (page 27). As you plate each omelette, place a full piece of burrata on the side of each omelette. Using a slotted spoon, evenly spoon the marinated tomatoes over each omelette and garnish with fresh basil leaves.

## INGREDIENTS & PREP

**Cherry Tomatoes** – 1½ pounds, halved lengthwise, heirloom variety

**Olive Oil** – ⅓ cup

**Sherry Vinegar** – 1½ tablespoons

**Garlic** – 1 clove, finely minced

**Red Pepper Flakes** – ½ teaspoon

**Sea Salt** – ¾ teaspoon

**Black Pepper** – ½ teaspoon, freshly cracked

**Burrata** – 4 pieces, 4 ounces each, at room temperature, divided

**Basil** – 1 cup, whole leaves, fresh, divided

—

*Serves 4*

## NOTES

# Deeply Roasted Garlic Omelette

AROMATIC GARLIC TURNS SWEET AND VELVETY AS IT ROASTS

## DIRECTIONS

1. Preheat oven to 400 degrees F.

2. Start by cutting ½-inch off the top of each head of garlic.

3. Place each head of garlic in the well of a muffin pan. Drizzle evenly with olive oil, making sure to rub the olive oil into the tops of the garlic cloves.

4. Cover with aluminum foil and bake for 30 – 40 minutes, until the garlic is golden brown.

5. Remove the garlic from the oven and allow to cool for 20 minutes.

6. Use a small fork to remove each garlic clove from the skin. Reserve any olive oil that has collected in the bottom of each muffin well.

7. Refer to my *Simple French Omelette* (page 27). Add to each of the four prep bowls 3 roughly chopped roasted garlic cloves. Follow my technique for cooking each omelette.

8. As you plate each omelette, top with a slice of triple cream brie, drizzle over a bit of the roasted garlic oil, and garnish each omelette with microgreens.

## INGREDIENTS & PREP

**Garlic** - 12 heads, medium size

**Olive Oil** - 1½ cups

**Triple Cream Brie Cheese** - 4 slices, ¼-inch thick, at room temperature

**Microgreens** - 1 cup, divided

—

*Makes 12 heads of roasted garlic*

**Tip:** Clearly this recipe for roasted garlic makes *way* more than you need for four omelettes. But once you taste the roasted sweet and velvety garlic cloves, these will be a staple in your refrigerator (welcome to the club!) to add to cheese boards, soups, salads, pastas, and anything that can use a deeply roasted garlicky kick! You can store them, out of their papery skins—in an airtight container for up to 7 days in the refrigerator. Any of the oil that collects in the bottom of each well should be used up within a few days. I mean, isn't that what a baguette is for—to "clean" the bottom of each muffin well of warm garlic oil?

# Homemade Herbed Goat Cheese Omelette

## TANGY CHEESE GETS AN HERBACEOUS MAKEOVER

### DIRECTIONS

① Add all of the ingredients, reserving the micro greens, into a medium bowl and stir until smooth. Set aside.

② Prepare my *Simple French Omelette* (page 27). As you plate each omelette, spread 2 tablespoons of the herbed goat cheese onto the top of each omelette and garnish with micro greens.

**Tip**: Pink pepper, while still spicy like black pepper, has a slight floral note and really brings out the flavor in the tangy goat cheese and fresh herbs. Pink peppercorns are very papery and grind very easily in a mortar and pestle or even in a small plastic bag and hit with a rolling pin (thanks nan for teaching me that trick with Graham crackers for making pie shells!).

**Idea**: Microgreens are an extremely versatile garnish. They add a crisp texture, bright green color, and freshness to plated dishes (and make even the simplest presentation look elevated)!

**Make Ahead**: This recipe calls for cloves of roasted garlic (page 37). Roasted garlic will last up to 1 week in an airtight container and stored in the refrigerator. Just allow the roasted garlic cloves to sit at room temperature for 30 minutes before adding them into the herbed goat cheese.

### INGREDIENTS & PREP

**Goat Cheese** – 5 ounces, at room temperature

**Chives** – 1 tablespoon, finely minced, fresh

**Dill** – 1 teaspoon, finely minced, fresh

**Parsley** – 1 tablespoon, finely minced, fresh, Italian flat-leaf variety

**Heavy Cream** – 5 tablespoons, at room temperature

**Pink Pepper** – ¾ teaspoon, freshly cracked

**Fleur de Sel** – ½ teaspoon

**Roasted Garlic** – 4 cloves, roughly chopped, page 37

**Microgreens** – 1 cup, divided

—

*Serves 4*

# Buttered Leeks & Zucchini Omelette

ONION-Y FLAVOR GIVES A BITE TO GARDEN-FRESH VEGETABLES

## DIRECTIONS

① In a medium sauté pan set over medium heat, add the butter and olive oil.  Once hot, add the leeks, zucchini, squash, salt, and pepper and cook for 5 minutes, stirring occasionally.

② Add the white wine and continue cooking for another 2 – 4 minutes, until the wine has reduced and the vegetables are tender.

③ Off the heat, stir in the lemon zest.  Set aside.

④ Prepare my *Simple French Omelette* (page 27).  As you plate each omelette, evenly top with fontina cheese and the warm buttered vegetables.  Scatter the fresh dill and parsley over to finish.

Tip:  Since you are going to open a bottle of wine for 3 tablespoons, make sure it is something you would drink.  I prefer a dry chardonnay that is crisp and oaky and that will add flavor to the vegetables.  If you would prefer to not add wine, simply leave it out and cook the vegetables for 6 – 8 minutes total.

## INGREDIENTS & PREP

**Butter** - 3 tablespoons, unsalted, French recommended

**Olive Oil** - 3 tablespoons

**Leeks** - 2 cups, thinly sliced, white and light green parts, cleaned of all sand

**Zucchini** - 1 small, ½-inch diced

**Yellow Squash** - 1 small, ½-inch diced

**Sea Salt** - 1 teaspoon

**Black Pepper** - ¾ teaspoon, freshly cracked

**White Wine** - 3 tablespoons, at room temperature, French chardonnay recommended

**Lemon Zest** - ¾ teaspoon, freshly zested

**Fontina Cheese** - ½ cup, divided, Fontina Val d'Aosta recommended

**Dill** - 4 tablespoons, whole fronds, fresh, divided

**Parsley** - tablespoons, whole leaves, fresh, Italian flat-leaf variety

—

*Serves 4*

# Omelette *au* Fromage

## ENDLESS POSSIBILITIES WITH CHEESE AWAIT YOU!

An omelette with cheese is a classic bistro staple in Paris, and around the world. There are endless possibilities when it comes to selecting a cheese to pair with my *Simple French Omelette* (page 27). There are a few things you need to keep in mind when topping your finished omelette. Here are a few of my tried-and-true tips:

**Temperature**—since I like putting cheese on top of my omelettes (sometimes putting cheese inside an omelette makes it too wet or runny), I like to use cheese that is at room temperature. I leave my pre-measured amounts of all varieties and types of cheese on the counter for at least 30 – 60 minutes. This allows the cheese to melt more quickly on the freshly made omelette and has more flavor than a straight-from-the-refrigerator cheese.

**Grated**—for all my recipes I always use freshly grated cheese. When you buy cheese that has been pre-grated, shredded, or shaved you can't know when it was processed, and it begins to lose its freshness and flavor well before you buy it. I use a simple box grater for most cheeses, a rasp if I want finely grated cheese, and even the food processor for Parmesan cheese (an Ina Garten tip!) when I want a more coarsely-ground texture.

**Soft Cheese**—when it comes to soft cheese like Boursin and other creamy cheeses, I just use a butter knife to spread across the top of each plated omelette—it really is that simple! For a brie I like slices ¼-inch thick and slightly overlap them on top of each omelette.

**Flavor**—the glorious thing about cheese is there is a never-ending variety available. The bad news, not every variety is good paired with an omelette. I stay away from cheese flavored with anything sweet like honey or fruit (a blueberry goat cheese omelette? I'll pass!). Instead, I stick to the basics from the grocery store and try local artisan cheeses from farmers markets. Buy small quantities of different types to discover what you like.

**Measurements**—is there ever enough cheese?! I find that most people prefer 1 tablespoon per omelette of stronger cheeses like Roquefort. That is just the right amount to add flavor without overpowering the dish. For milder cheeses like Fontina about 2 tablespoons does just the trick. The goal isn't for the omelette to be covered in a gluttonous amount of cheese but to have enough for flavor and texture (and maybe a *bit* decadent!).

# Roasted Vine Tomato & Parmesan Omelette
## IS THERE ANYTHING BETTER THAN PERFECTLY ROASTED TOMATOES?

### DIRECTIONS

1. Preheat the oven to 350 degrees F.

2. Place the stem of tomatoes onto a half sheet pan and drizzle with olive oil and sprinkle with salt and pepper.

3. Roast for 10 – 15 minutes, until the tomatoes are wilted but not bursting. Set aside.

4. Prepare my *Simple French Omelette* (page 27). As you plate each omelette, top each one with Parmesan cheese, a stem of warm roasted tomatoes and scatter over with fresh basil and parsley leaves.

### INGREDIENTS & PREP

Vine Tomatoes - 4 stems (plus any that fall off the vine)

Olive Oil - ½ cup

Sea Salt - 1 teaspoon

Black Pepper - 1 teaspoon, freshly cracked

Parmesan Cheese - 1 cup, freshly grated, divided, Parmigiano-Reggiano recommended

Basil - ½ cup, whole leaves, fresh, divided

Parsley - ½ cup, whole leaves, fresh, divided

—

*Serves 4*

**Tip:** Even when it isn't tomato season, you can make this omelette all year round. Stems of cocktail tomatoes are easily found at most grocery stores. In fact, they can range from the size of a nickel to a half dollar! If you can only find smaller vine tomatoes, start with roasting for 5 – 7 minutes, just keep your eye on them. If you can only find larger ones, you may have to increase the overall roasting time. In this case, size doesn't matter (well, that's another book!).

### NOTES

_____

_____

_____

_____

_____

_____

_____

# Sweet Corn & White Cheddar Omelette

## A NOD TO MY NEW ENGLAND ROOTS

### DIRECTIONS

① In a medium sauté pan set over medium heat, add the butter and heavy cream. Once hot, add the corn kernels.

② Cook for 3 – 5 minutes, stirring occasionally, until the corn is tender but still crisp.

③ Prepare my *Simple French Omelette* (page 27). As you plate each omelette, top evenly with grated cheddar and then with warm corn. Sprinkle over with fleur de sel to taste, and scatter over with fresh basil leaves.

Tip: I always make this omelette when the farmers markets and farm stands are filled with fresh sweet corn. Corn was, and still is, my favorite thing about summer! But, you can make this omelette year-round—just use frozen corn that has been defrosted at room temperature for at least 30 minutes.

### INGREDIENTS & PREP

Butter - 1 tablespoon, unsalted, French recommended

Heavy Cream - 3 tablespoons

Sweet Corn - 1¼ cups, whole kernels

Sea Salt - ¼ teaspoon

Black Pepper - ¼ teaspoon, freshly cracked

English Cheddar - ½ cup, freshly grated, at room temperature, divided

Fleur de Sel - for garnish

Basil - 1 cup, whole leaves, fresh

—

*Serves 4*

### NOTES

_____

_____

_____

_____

_____

_____

_____

# The 808 Omelette

SRIRACHA-ROASTED BROCCOLI & BASIL ADD A CHINATOWN FLAIR

## DIRECTIONS

① Preheat the oven to 400 degrees F.

② In a small bowl, whisk together the olive oil, Sriracha, salt, and pepper. In a separate small bowl toss together the avocado and lemon juice. Set both aside.

③ Add the broccoli to a half sheet pan and drizzle over the olive oil mixture. Toss to evenly coat. Roast for 12 – 15 minutes, tossing once halfway through, until the broccoli is crisp-tender.

④ Next, to the sheet pan, add the lemon zest, basil, and green onions. Toss everything together and allow to sit at room temperature for just a few minutes.

⑤ Prepare my *Simple French Omelette* (page 27). As you plate each omelette, top each one with the warm roasted broccoli mixture and avocado. Garnish with fleur de sel.

## INGREDIENTS & PREP

Olive Oil - ¼ cup

Sriracha - 2 tablespoons

Sea Salt - ½ teaspoon

Black Pepper - ½ teaspoon

Avocado - 1 large, ¼-inch diced, Haas variety

Lemon Juice - 1 tablespoon, freshly squeezed

Broccoli - 12 ounces, florets only

Lemon Zest - 1 teaspoon

Basil - 1 cup, whole leaves, fresh

Green Onion - 4 tablespoons, thinly sliced, white and light green parts

Fleur de Sel - for garnish

—

*Serves 4*

Note: Our best friends live in Hawaii, which uses the area code 808 and we visit them whenever we can. They live near Chinatown and in the mornings, I love to go for a walk and see all of the open-air stalls at the street markets. There was a little pho restaurant that we would go to over and over again while visiting. They had the best bowls of steaming noodles and the owner would always add basil, broccoli, and lemon zest to mine. It has since closed, but those were unforgettable flavors and *The 808 Omelette* came from my inspiration. Now if only I would invent a recipe to combat jet lag!

# Million Dollar Omelette
## A TASTE OF THE LUXE LIFE

## DIRECTIONS

*CRÈME FRAÎCHE SAUCE*

1. Place all of the ingredients into a small bowl and whisk together until smooth. Transfer it into a small pitcher or silver bowl with a spoon. Set aside.

*MILLION DOLLAR OMELETTE*

2. Prepare my *Simple French Omelette* (page 27) except substitute the unsalted butter for each omelette with 1 tablespoon of truffle butter.

3. As you plate each omelette, garnish with a sprinkling of truffle salt, microgreens, truffle carpaccio, and gold leaf. Serve with the Crème Fraîche Sauce on the side.

**Tip:** If you really want to amp up the luxe factor, shave fresh Urbani black truffles onto each plate tableside—it makes for a very dramatic and luxurious experience and will fill the dining room with the intoxicating smell of fresh truffles!

## NOTES

## INGREDIENTS & PREP

*CRÈME FRAÎCHE SAUCE*

**Crème Fraîche** - ¾ cup, at room temperature

**Heavy Cream** - 2 tablespoons

**Parmesan Cheese** - 4 tablespoons, very finely grated (on a rasp or microplane)

**Fleur de Sel** - ¼ teaspoon

**Black Pepper** - ¼ teaspoon, freshly cracked

*COMPONENTS*

**White Truffle Butter** - 4 tablespoons, Urbani recommended

**Truffle Salt** - for garnish, Urbani recommended

**Microgreens** - 1 cup, divided, for garnish

**Summer Black Truffles Carpaccio** - 4 ounces, divided, Urbani recommended

**Edible Gold Leaf** - for garnish

—

*Serves 4*

# White Bean & Fennel Ragu Omelette

A SOUL-SATISFYING DISH FILLED WITH FAMILIAR & COMPLEX FLAVORS

## DIRECTIONS

1. Preheat the oven to 350 degrees F.

2. In a 3½-quart covered baking dish, like a Dutch oven, add all of the ingredients, reserving the parmesan cheese and white beans, and stir to combine, making sure to nestle the parsley down into the vegetables.

3. Bake for 40 minutes, stir, and continue baking for another 40 minutes with the lid slightly ajar.

4. Remove the pan from the oven, stir in the parmesan cheese and white beans. Cover and allow it to sit for 10 minutes.

5. Prepare my *Simple French Omelette* (page 27). Before you plate each omelette, spoon 1 cup of the ragu into the center of each plate and place each finished omelette on top. Garnish with more whole fresh parsley leaves.

Make Ahead: This recipe makes more than enough to serve alongside 4 omelettes. It will last in the refrigerator in an airtight container for up to 5 days (gently reheat it in a sauté pan set over medium heat), making leftovers perfect to enjoy on toasted baguette slices as an hors d'oeuvre or served as a topping on a tartine and green salad—just garnish it with more fresh parsley and guests will think you whipped it up minutes before they arrived!

## INGREDIENTS & PREP

Fennel - 1 cup, ¼-inch diced

Red Onion - 1 cup, ¼-inch diced

Yellow Squash - 1 cup, ¼-inch diced

Graffiti Eggplant - 1 cup, ¼-inch diced

Red Pepper - 1 cup, ¼-inch diced

Garlic - 1 clove, finely minced

Sun-Dried Tomatoes - 4 tablespoons, roughly chopped, packed in oil

Tomato - 1 can (28 ounces), whole tomatoes

Parsley - 5 sprigs, tied together with kitchen string, fresh, plus more for garnish, Italian flat-leaf variety

Olive Oil - 3 tablespoons

Sea Salt - 1 teaspoon

Black Pepper - ¾ teaspoon, freshly cracked

Parmesan Cheese - ½ cup, freshly grated, Parmigiano-Reggiano recommended

White Beans - 1 can (15 ounces), rinsed and drained

—

*Serves 4*

# French Feta & Sun-Dried Tomato Omelette

A FRENCH-INSPIRED VERSION OF A MEDITERRANEAN OMELET

## DIRECTIONS

① Prepare my *Simple French Omelettes* (page 27). As you plate each omelette, top each one evenly with feta, oregano, sun-dried tomatoes, and arugula. Garnish with fleur de sel and pepper.

**Serving Idea**: The oil that the sun-dried tomatoes are packed in has such intense flavor! I like to drizzle a little over the omelettes—not only does it add more flavor but adds amazing color. You can even toss a few tablespoons of the oil with arugula and shavings of parmesan for a fast and incredibly chic salad. Whatever you do, make sure you don't waste a single drop!

**Tip**: In order to get as much flavor out of the dried oregano as possible, rub it between the palms of your hands over each omelette. This will help release the remaining essential oils that are left in the leaves. Remember—dried herbs have a shelf life, so make sure that your oregano still smells like oregano when you open the bottle (and it isn't from 1978!).

## INGREDIENTS & PREP

**French Feta** – 8 ounces, ¼-inch diced, at room temperature, divided

**Oregano** – 1 teaspoon, dried, divided

**Sun-Dried Tomatoes** – ¾ cup, packed in oil variety, divided

**Arugula** – 1 cup, divided

**Fleur de Sel** – for garnish

**Black Pepper** – freshly cracked, for garnish

—

*Serves 4*

## NOTES

_____

_____

_____

_____

_____

_____

_____

_____

# Saffron Omelette

## THE HUMBLE EGG GETS AN EXOTIC TWIST

### DIRECTIONS

① Prepare my *Simple French Omelette* (page 27). As you melt each tablespoon of butter, add ½ teaspoon of saffron threads and allow the butter to melt and become infused with the spicy and vibrant spice. Continue to follow my technique for cooking each omelette.

② As you plate each omelette, garnish with a few more threads of saffron, fleur de sel, and microgreens.

**Tip:** Saffron threads, which are the stamens of the crocus flower, are hand-harvested during a one-week period each year, making this the most expensive spice in the world. Most larger grocery stores sell it in the spice aisle, and you can find it in spice shops, multi-cultural grocery stores, and online. This particular omelette is also a great candidate to add a little shine with edible gold leaf as a garnish. Edible gold leaf is the new "little black dress"—it will never go out of style (and something your guests will not expect)!

### INGREDIENTS & PREP

**Saffron** - 2 teaspoons, divided, plus more for garnish

**Fleur de Sel** - for garnish

**Microgreens** - 1 cup, divided

—

*Serves 4*

### NOTES

# Sheet Pan Omelette

## FROM OVEN TO TABLE—A ONE-SHEET WONDER

### DIRECTIONS

① Preheat the oven to 400 degrees F.

② Add the asparagus, green onions, garlic, olive oil, salt, and pepper to a half sheet pan and toss together. Arrange everything to be in a single layer.

③ Roast for 8 – 10 minutes, depending on the thickness of the asparagus, until crisp-tender. Sprinkle over the Parmesan cheese, return the pan back to the oven, and cook another 1 – 2 minutes, until the cheese is just melted.

④ Prepare my *Simple French Omelette* (page 27). Arrange each finished omelette on top of the roasted asparagus and green onions. Top each omelette with an equal amount of Gruyère cheese and scatter over your choice of greens and all of the fresh herbs. Serve tableside with my *Everyday Lemon Vinaigrette* and allow guests to add as much vinaigrette as desired.

### INGREDIENTS & PREP

**Asparagus** - 12 ounces, ends trimmed

**Green Onion** - 5 stalked, ends trimmed, cut in half lengthwise

**Garlic** - 2 cloves, finely minced

**Olive** - ¼ cup

**Sea Salt** - ½ teaspoon

**Black Pepper** - ½ teaspoon, freshly cracked

**Parmesan Cheese** - ½ cup, freshly grated, Parmigiano-Reggiano recommended

**Gruyère Cheese** - 4 tablespoons, freshly grated, at room temperature

**Greens** - 2 cups, divided, spring mix or arugula recommended

**Basil** - ¼ cup, whole leaves, fresh

**Dill** - ¼ cup, whole fronds, fresh

**Parsley** - ¼ cup, whole leaves, fresh

**Tarragon** - ¼ cup, whole leaves, fresh

**Chives** - ½ cup, cut to 1-inch lengths

*Everyday Lemon Vinaigrette* - page 103

—

*Serves 4*

# Fines Herbes Omelette

A BISTRO CLASSIC FOR ANYTIME-OF-DAY ENTERTAINING

## DIRECTIONS

① Refer to my *Simple French Omelette* (page 27). To the 4 prep bowls add ¾-teaspoon each of the fresh herbs. Follow my technique for cooking and plating each omelette.

**Tip**: A traditional fines herbes French omelette calls for chervil, which is in the parsley family. It isn't a common grocery store herb, so I use Italian flat-leaf parsley instead. If you want to experiment with other herbs, stick to tender and leafy herbs like basil, thyme, carrot fronds, fennel fronds, or chive flowers (they make a fabulous garnish if you can find them or grow them!), really any herb that is tender and has great flavor. Rosemary, however, is really too woody in an omelette and is best when sautéed, roasted, or cooked to help soften up the leaves. Of course, you can always try my *Rosemary & Thyme Butter Omelette* on page 81 for that spicy and earthy kick from rosemary!

## INGREDIENTS & PREP

**Dill** - 3 teaspoons, fresh, finely minced, divided

**Tarragon** - 3 teaspoons, fresh, finely minced, divided

**Chives** - 3 teaspoons, fresh, finely minced, divided

**Parsley** - 3 teaspoons, fresh, finely minced, divided, Italian flat-leaf variety

—

*Serves 4*

**Entertaining Idea**: Don't be afraid to experiment with adding cheese to each omelette. Typically, my omelette recipes call for between one and two tablespoons of cheese, always at room temperature—so have your own culinary adventure. I've never known a slice of melting triple cream brie to make anything taste worse!

## NOTES

_____

_____

_____

_____

_____

_____

# French Onion Soup Omelette

RYAN'S FAVORITE OMELETTE OF ALL TIME!

## DIRECTIONS

① In a 10-inch sauté pan set over medium-low heat, add the olive oil and 2 tablespoons of butter. Once hot, add the onions, salt, and pepper. Cook for 30 minutes, stirring occasionally, until the onions are very soft and caramelized.

② Next, turn the heat to low, and add the remaining 2 tablespoons of butter. Continue cooking for another 5 minutes.

③ Lastly, add the white wine and continue cooking for another 2 minutes, scraping the browned bits from the bottom of the pan. Set aside.

④ Prepare my *Simple French Omelette* (page 27). As you plate each omelette, top each one evenly with Gruyère cheese, warm caramelized onions, Baguette Crumbs, and finally with fresh parsley leaves.

**Tip**: The onions can be made up to 3 days ahead of time and stored in an airtight container in the refrigerator. Slowly warm them up in a medium sauté pan set over low heat with a tablespoon of unsalted butter. I always check for seasonings when reheating anything that was made in advance, so a pinch of fleur de sel and more black pepper may be necessary.

## INGREDIENTS & PREP

Olive Oil - ¼ cup

Butter - 4 tablespoons, unsalted, divided, French recommended

Onions - 4 cups, thinly sliced, a combination of red and yellow

Sea Salt - 1 teaspoon

Black Pepper - ¾ teaspoon, freshly cracked

White Wine - 3 tablespoons, French Chardonnay recommended

Gruyère Cheese - 1 cup, freshly grated, divided, at room temperature

Parsley - 1 cup, whole leaves, fresh, Italian flat-leaf variety

*Baguette Crumbs* - page 69

—

*Serves 4*

# Roasted Fennel & Parmesan Omelette
## A PERFECT COMBINATION WITH A GLASS OF CRISP ROSÉ

### DIRECTIONS

① Preheat the oven to 400 degrees F.

② Remove the stems of the fennel and slice the bulb in half lengthwise. With the cut side down, slice the bulb vertically into ½-inch-thick slices, cutting right through the core so that you end up with wedges.

③ Place the fennel onto a half sheet pan and toss with olive oil, salt and pepper.

④ Roast for 10 minutes, toss and continue roasting for another 10 – 15 minutes or until golden brown.

⑤ Prepare my *Simple French Omelette* (page 27). As you plate each omelette, top each one with roasted fennel, shavings of Parmesan cheese, parsley, and tarragon.

### INGREDIENTS & PREP

**Fennel** - 2 large bulbs

**Olive Oil** - ¼ cup

**Sea Salt** - ¾ teaspoon

**Black Pepper** - ½ teaspoon, freshly cracked

**Parmesan Cheese** - 2 cups, large shavings, divided, Parmigiano-Reggiano recommended

**Parsley** - ¼ cup, whole leaves, fresh divided, Italian flat-leaf variety

**Tarragon** - ¼ cup, whole leaves, fresh, divided

—

*Serves 4*

**Tip:** Fennel fronds also make a fabulous garnish—just make sure they are not wilted. You can also add the fennel stems to homemade vegetable stock or into a pot of risotto as it cooks to add some anise flavor.

### NOTES

# Asparagus Omelette *with* Truffle Oil
## A DRIZZLE OF TRUFFLE OIL & LOTS OF FONTINA GOES A LONG WAY

### DIRECTIONS

1. Preheat the oven to 400 degrees F.

2. Add the asparagus, garlic, olive oil, salt and pepper to a half sheet pan and toss together. Arrange the asparagus in a single layer.

3. Roast for 8 – 10 minutes, depending on the thickness of the stalks, until crisp-tender.

4. Prepare my *Simple French Omelette* (page 27). As you plate each omelette, top with even amounts of Fontina cheese and truffle oil. Add a bundle of the roasted asparagus to each omelette and scatter over parsley leaves. Garnish with fleur de sel and more black pepper.

### INGREDIENTS & PREP

**Asparagus** - 12 ounces, ends trimmed

**Garlic** - 2 cloves, finely minced

**Olive Oil** - 3 tablespoons

**Sea Salt** - 1 teaspoon

**Black Pepper** - 1 teaspoon, freshly cracked

**Fontina Cheese** - ½ cup, freshly shredded, at room temperature, divided, Fontina Val d'Aosta recommended

**Truffle Oil** - 4 tablespoons, divided, Urbani recommended

**Parsley** - ½ cup, whole leaves, fresh, divided, Italian flat-leaf variety

**Fleur de Sel** - for garnish

—

*Serves 4*

### NOTES

# Crème Fraîche Omelette

BAGUETTE CRUMBS & PARSLEY DRESS THIS FOR COCKTAIL HOUR

## DIRECTIONS

①  Line a half sheet pan with parchment paper. Set aside.

②  In the bowl of a food processor fitted with a steel blade, add the cubed bread. Pulse until you get coarse bread crumbs. Set aside.

③  In a medium sauté pan set over medium heat, add the butter, olive oil, and garlic cloves. Once hot, add the bread crumbs and toast for 6 – 8 minutes, tossing occasionally until the crumbs are golden brown. Discard the garlic cloves.

④  Off the heat, add the salt and pepper, and toss to combine. Pour the breadcrumbs, in a single layer, onto the prepared half sheet pan and allow to cool for 5 minutes.

⑤  Prepare my *Simple French Omelette* (page 27). As each omelette is finished cooking, transfer it to a cutting board. Slice it into small bite-sized pieces and place each piece onto a tasting spoon, then place the spoon onto a serving tray. Add a little dollop of crème fraîche, a sprinkling of Baguette Crumbs, and a fresh parsley leaf.

Tip:  I give you full permission to garnish any omelette in this book with Baguette Crumbs (and also eat them by the spoonful out of the pan while they are still hot!).

## INGREDIENTS & PREP

**French Baguette** - 6 ounces, 1-inch cubed

**Butter** - 3 tablespoons, unsalted, French recommended

**Olive Oil** - 2 tablespoons

**Garlic** - 2 cloves, lightly crushed (using the broadside of your knife)

**Fleur de Sel** - ½ teaspoon

**Black Pepper** - ½ teaspoon, freshly cracked

**Crème Fraîche** - ½ cup, at room temperature, divided

**Parsley** - 1 cup, whole leaves, fresh, divided, Italian flat-leaf variety

—

*Serves 4*

**Entertaining Idea**:  Of course, you can serve this omelette in its full-size (plate each omelette and top with crème fraîche, Baguette Crumbs, and parsley), but when you serve it cocktail-soirée style, people go crazy! I found these little silver spoons at E.Dehillerin in Paris for just a few euros. But you can find tasting spoons online—silver, white porcelain, bamboo, and even ones with pretty patterns. Don't be afraid to use simple tablespoons—your guests will be ecstatic you cooked for them and took the time to present this omelette so beautifully!

# Herbes *de* Provence Omelette

A MÉLANGE OF SAVORY AND FLORAL NOTES

## DIRECTIONS

① Add the dried herbes de provence to a mortar and pestle. Gently press onto the dried herbs to help release their flavor. If you don't have a mortar and pestle, place the dried herbs on your cutting board and use the back of a spoon to approximate the same technique.

② Next, add 1 tablespoon of parsley to each prep bowl for my *Simple French Omelette* (page 27).

③ As you add 1 tablespoon of butter to the pan for each omelette, also add 1 teaspoon of herbes de provence. Continue cooking each omelette as directed on page 27.

④ As you plate each omelette, sprinkle over 1 tablespoon of Parmesan cheese. Top each omelette with your choice of greens lightly dressed in my *French Bistro Vinaigrette*.

**Tip**: Herbes de provence is traditionally a blend of thyme, basil, savory, fennel, and lavender that captures the flavors of the sunny French countryside of Provence. It is very fragrant and adds a real depth of flavor to this omelette. The dried lavender gives it a slight floral note while the fresh parsley helps bring out the other savory herbs.

## INGREDIENTS & PREP

**Herbes de Provence** - 4 teaspoons, divided

**Parsley** - 4 tablespoons, roughly chopped, divided, Italian flat-leaf variety

**Parmesan Cheese** - 4 tablespoons, freshly grated, at room temperature, Parmigiano-Reggiano recommended

**Greens** - 5 ounces, spring mix or baby arugula recommended

*French Bistro Vinaigrette* - for dressing greens, page 115

—

*Serves 4*

# Lemon Zest Omelette

## AN UNEXPECTED CITRUS TWIST

### DIRECTIONS

1. Refer to my *Simple French Omelette* (page 27). To the 4 prep bowls, add 1 teaspoon each of the lemon zest. Follow my technique for cooking each omelette.

2. As you plate each omelette, garnish with a shaving of Parmesan cheese, fresh basil, and more black pepper.

**Tip**: Lemon zest adds such a zing to eggs and really awakens their flavor. If you are going to serve a green salad as an accompaniment, choose my *Vinaigrette Vert* (page 109) to dress cold crisp arugula—the spicy Parmesan and peppery arugula with the lemony omelette are a match made in flavor heaven!

### INGREDIENTS & PREP

**Lemon Zest** - 4 teaspoons, freshly grated, divided

**Parmesan Cheese** - ½ cup, large shavings, Parmigiano-Reggiano recommended

**Basil** - 4 tablespoons, julienned, divided

**Black Pepper** - freshly cracked, for garnish

—

*Serves 4*

### NOTES

_____

_____

_____

_____

_____

_____

_____

# Confetti Corn Omelette

## A COLORFUL CONCOCTION OF IN-SEASON VEGETABLES

### DIRECTIONS

① In a small bowl, add the avocado and lemon juice and gently stir, being careful not to break up the avocado. Set aside.

② In a medium sauté pan set over medium-low heat, add the olive oil. Once hot, add the corn, red peppers, jalapeño, salt, and pepper. Cook for 3 – 5 minutes, until the corn and peppers are crisp-tender, stirring occasionally.

③ Transfer to a serving bowl and add the green onions, Parmesan cheese, basil, and avocados. Gently stir to combine.

④ Prepare my *Simple French Omelette* (page 27). As you plate each omelette, top each one with a generous spoonful of the corn mixture. Garnish with more salt, pepper, Parmesan cheese, and fresh basil.

**Tip:** Most of my recipes call for leafy herbs, like basil, to be roughly chopped. In this case I think julienned (also known as chiffonade) basil looks more elevated, and it couldn't be easier. Simply stack the basil leaves, roll them up (as though into a cigar shape), and using a sharp knife make long, thin cuts crosswise. You will end up with thin and elegant strands that only take seconds to cut!

### INGREDIENTS & PREP

**Avocado** - 1 large, ¼-inch diced, Haas variety

**Lemon Juice** - 1 tablespoon, freshly squeezed

**Olive Oil** - 4 tablespoons

**Sweet Corn** - 2 cups, whole kernels

**Red Pepper** - 1 large, ¼-inch diced

**Jalapeño** - 1 small, seeded, finely minced

**Sea Salt** - ¾ teaspoon

**Black Pepper** - ½ teaspoon, freshly cracked

**Green Onion** - 2 stalks, thinly sliced, white and light green parts

**Parmesan Cheese** - ¼ cup, freshly grated, plus more for garnish, Parmigiano-Reggiano recommended

**Basil** - 4 tablespoons, julienned, fresh, plus more for garnish

—

*Serves 4*

# Endive & Roquefort Omelette

## CRUNCHY, CREAMY, AND PERFECTLY SEASONED

### DIRECTIONS

① In a medium sauté pan set over medium-low heat, add butter and olive oil. Once hot, add the endive, salt, pepper, and sugar. Cook for 10 – 12 minutes, stirring occasionally, until the endive is caramelized.

② Next, add the garlic and thyme. Cook for another 1 – 2 minutes, being careful not to burn the garlic.

③ Add the white wine and allow it to reduce for 2 – 3 minutes, until most of the liquid is gone, scraping up any browned bits in the pan. Set aside.

④ Prepare my *Simple French Omelette* (page 27). As you plate each omelette, top each one with the endive mixture, 1 tablespoon of Roquefort, chives, and fleur de sel.

### INGREDIENTS & PREP

**Butter** - 3 tablespoons, unsalted, French recommended

**Olive Oil** - 2 tablespoons

**Endive** - 6 heads, cored, ½-inch diced

**Sea Salt** - ½ teaspoon

**Black Pepper** - ¼ teaspoon, freshly cracked

**Sugar** - ½ teaspoon, granulated

**Garlic** - 1 clove, finely minced

**Thyme** - 1 teaspoon, fresh, finely minced

**White Wine** - 3 tablespoons, French chardonnay, at room temperature

**Roquefort Cheese** - 4 ounces, crumbled, divided, at room temperature

**Chives** - 1 cup, fresh, cut to 1-inch lengths, divided

**Fleur de Sel** - for garnish

—

*Serves 4*

### NOTES

_____

_____

_____

_____

_____

_____

_____

# Balsamic Red Pepper Omelette *with* Fontina

## A SHARP, VINEGARY BITE WITH A TOUCH OF SWEET RED PEPPER

### DIRECTIONS

1. In a medium bowl, add the roasted red peppers, balsamic vinegar, smoked paprika, red pepper flakes, salt, and pepper, and stir to combine. Allow to sit at room temperature for 30 minutes.

2. Prepare my *Simple French Omelette* (page 27). As you plate each omelette, evenly top with Fontina and Parmesan cheese.

3. Using a slotted spoon, evenly spoon over the marinated roasted red pepper mixture and garnish each omelette with fresh basil.

Tip: When selecting Fontina cheese, look for Italian Fontina Val d'Aosta. It has so much more richness and flavor than its Danish cousin (which has a red wax rind), and has a fudgy, creamy texture that melts like a dream!

### INGREDIENTS & PREP

Roasted Red Peppers – 1 jar (12 ounces), drained, ¼-inch diced

Balsamic Vinegar – 1½ tablespoons

Smoked Paprika – ½ teaspoon

Red Pepper Flakes – ¼ teaspoon

Sea Salt – ¼ teaspoon

Black Pepper – ¼ teaspoon, freshly cracked

Fontina Cheese – 4 ounces, freshly grated, at room temperature, divided, Fontina Val d'Aosta recommended

Parmesan Cheese – 4 tablespoons, at room temperature, freshly grated, divided, Parmigiano-Reggiano recommended

Basil – ½ cup, whole leaves, fresh, divided

—

*Serves 4*

### NOTES

# Rosemary & Thyme Butter Omelette

HERB BUNDLE + WARM BUTTER = A HEAVENLY-SMELLING KITCHEN

## DIRECTIONS

① Start by placing a 10-inch length of kitchen twine on your work surface. Stack the herbs on top of the twine so that stems are parallel to each other. Tie the twine around the herbs to bundle them together. Knot to secure.

② Place the fresh herb bundle into the pan and allow each tablespoon of butter (per *Simple French Omelette*, page 27) to melt and be infused by the herbs.

③ Once the herbs start to pop, remove the bundle, place it onto a small plate, add the eggs, and continue the cooking process.

④ Repeat these steps for the remaining omelettes.

**Entertaining Idea:** This is such an earthy way of cooking and fills the kitchen with beautiful aromas of fresh herbs and melting butter—does it get any better?! Whenever I serve this particular omelette, I make extra herb bundles and leave them on each guest place setting for them to take home as a little something to remember the evening. I even use fresh herbs in little juice glasses as "flowers" for the table. Thoughtful details versus grand gestures, are what people will always remember.

## INGREDIENTS & PREP

**Rosemary** - 5 sprigs, fresh
**Thyme** - 5 sprigs, fresh
**Kitchen Twine** - 10 inches
—

*Serves 4*

# Butter & Thyme Roasted Radish Omelette

SPICY RADISHES BATHED IN HERB-INFUSED BUTTER

## DIRECTIONS

① Preheat the oven to 400 degrees F.

② In an 8 x 10 x 2-inch baking dish, add all of the ingredients, reserving the butter and Parmesan cheese, and toss to combine.  Scatter the cold butter over the radishes.

③ Roast for 15 minutes, toss, and continue roasting for another 15 – 20 minutes until the radishes are tender and golden brown.  During the last 5 minutes of cooking, sprinkle over the Parmesan cheese.

④ Prepare my *Simple French Omelette* (page 27). As you plate each omelette, divide and scatter the radishes over each omelette.  Drizzle over any olive oil and butter left in the baking dish. Garnish each plate with whole thyme leaves, salt, and pepper.

Tip: Radishes come in a variety of types, colors, and sizes (I try to find heirloom varieties).  To ensure they roast evenly I cut the larger ones in quarters, the medium ones in half, and leave the smaller ones whole.  I love the mix of colors and shapes—it makes for an especially earthy presentation.

## INGREDIENTS & PREP

**Radishes** - 1 pound, trimmed and scrubbed

**Olive Oil** - 4 tablespoons

**Thyme** - 7 sprigs, fresh, plus more for garnish

**Sea Salt** - 1 teaspoon

**Black Pepper** - 1 teaspoon, freshly cracked

**Butter** - 6 tablespoons, unsalted, cold, French recommended

**Parmesan Cheese** - 4 tablespoons, freshly grated, at room temperature, Parmigiano-Reggiano recommended

—

*Serves 4*

# Gâteau *d'*Omelette

AN EARTHY AND ELEGANT TABLESIDE SHOWSTOPPER

## DIRECTIONS

① Choose a serving platter—something round—at least 12 inches in diameter. Set aside.

② In a large sauté pan set over medium-low heat, add the olive oil and 3 tablespoons of butter. Once hot, add the onions, salt, and pepper. Cook for 30 minutes, stirring occasionally, until the onions are very soft and caramelized.

③ Next, turn the heat to low and add the remaining 3 tablespoons of butter. Continue cooking for another 5 minutes. Lastly, add the white wine and cook for another 2 – 3 minutes, scraping up the browned bits from the pan. Set aside.

④ Refer to my *Simple French Omelette* recipe (page 27, you will be making a total of 8 unfolded omelettes—plan your ingredients accordingly). At step 5, instead of jerking to fold, slide the unfolded omelette directly into the center of your serving platter as the first layer. Repeat the same process 2 more times, layering each unfolded omelette.

⑤ Top the third layer with Gruyère cheese, parsley, arugula, and a sprinkling of Baguette Crumbs, making sure to reserve enough of these ingredients for the remaining 5 layers. Repeat this same process 5 more times, until all 5 layers have been garnished. After garnishing the final eighth layer, scatter over the microgreens.

## INGREDIENTS & PREP

**Olive Oil** - ½ cup

**Butter** - 6 tablespoons, unsalted, divided, French recommended

**Onions** - 8 cups, thinly sliced, a combination of red and yellow

**Sea Salt** - 2 teaspoons

**Black Pepper** - 1½ teaspoons, freshly cracked

**White Wine** - ½ cup, French chardonnay recommended

**Gruyère Cheese** - 1 cup, freshly grated, divided, at room temperature

**Parsley** - 1 cup, whole leaves, fresh, divided, Italian flat-leaf variety

**Baby Arugula** - 2 cups, divided

*Baguette Crumbs* - page 69, divided

**Microgreens** - ½ cup, divided

*Serves 6 - 8*

**Entertaining Tip**: To serve my show-stopping *Gâteau d'Omelette*, I like to use a very sharp knife to slice it as you would a cake—having a pie server to help transfer each slice from the serving platter to each plate makes it a lot easier. And speaking of easy, I promise you this recipe isn't difficult to make—in fact, the longest process is waiting for the onions to cook. It can also be made 30 minutes in advance and served warm.

basil from Raspail market

Apple tart from Poilâne Bakery

Adriane M.
Fleuriste Paris

Café life in the 5th

*Juliet balcony in the kitchen*

Ingredients from La Grande Epicerie de Paris

My Parisian
kitchen picnic

*Just after filming*
*'My Paris Adventure'*

My favorite baguette on
a flea market platter

Testing my
Creamy Roasted Potatoes

*le déjeuner*

Paul Bert Serpette
flea market

# Component Recipes

## EARTHY AND ELEGANT COMPLIMENTS FOR YOUR HOUSE MEAL

*"Dinner parties do not have to be about preparing course after course, getting up and down every ten minutes and driving yourself crazy making sure things are perfect—I would much rather sit with you and have my leg fall asleep, eat too much cheese, and lose count of the opened bottles of wine!"*

—Marc J. Sievers

# Warm Citrus & Herb Marinated Olives

## A NEW (AND QUICK!) TAKE ON COCKTAIL HOUR NIBBLES

### DIRECTIONS

① In a medium bowl, squeeze the orange and lemon wedges to get as much juice out of each wedge as possible. Add the squeezed wedges to the bowl along with all of the other ingredients, reserving the parsley and fleur de sel, and toss to combine. Allow the olive mixture to sit at room temperature for 20 minutes.

② Next, in a 10-inch sauté pan set over medium heat, transfer the mixture, including all the liquid. Once the oil begins to sizzle, lower the heat and sauté for 5 – 7 minutes, stirring occasionally, until the olives are warm and the tomatoes are soft.

③ Strain the mixture and transfer it to a serving bowl accompanied by a little side dish for the olive pits. Drizzle over 2 tablespoons of the hot liquid. Garnish with parsley and a generous sprinkling of fleur de sel. Serve warm.

**Tip:** Once you have removed the two tablespoons of liquid for serving, add 1 teaspoon of honey to the remaining warm liquid and whisk vigorously—an instant vinaigrette to accompany your meal! Allow it to cool before dressing a salad. I love this with cold, crisp arugula, big shavings of Parmesan cheese and my Brioche Croutons (page 103).

### INGREDIENTS & PREP

**Orange** - 1 large, cut into 8 wedges

**Lemon** - 1 large, cut into 8 wedges

**Olive Oil** - ⅔ cup

**Sherry Vinegar** - ¼ cup

**Garlic** - 4 cloves, peeled and smashed

**Thyme** - 7 sprigs, fresh

**Rosemary** - 2 sprigs, fresh

**Herbes de Provence** - 2 teaspoons, lightly crushed

**Red Pepper Flakes** - ½ teaspoon

**Sea Salt** - 1 teaspoon

**Black Pepper** - 1 teaspoon, freshly cracked

**Green Olives** - 2 cups, Cerignola variety

**Cherry Tomatoes** - 2 cups, heirloom variety

**Parsley** - 2 tablespoons, fresh, roughly chopped, Italian flat-leaf variety

**Fleur de Sel** - for garnish

—

*Serves 4*

# Everyday Lemon Vinaigrette

### YOUR HIGH-FLAVOR, LOW-EFFORT GO-TO DRESSING

## DIRECTIONS

### LEMON VINAIGRETTE

① Place all of the ingredients into a jar with a tight-fitting lid. Shake vigorously for about 60 seconds until the vinaigrette is well-blended.

**Tip:** This is by far my favorite lemon vinaigrette and one that I always have in the refrigerator. The flavor is sharp from the lemon, with just a hint of sweetness from the honey. It can be prepared up to 5 days in advance and stored in the same jar in which it was made.

### BRIOCHE CROUTONS

② Line a half sheet pan with parchment paper. Set aside.

③ In a medium sauté pan set over medium heat, add the butter. Once melted, add the brioche, fleur de sel, and pepper. Sauté for 4 – 6 minutes until golden brown, tossing often.

④ Transfer to the prepared half sheet pan to cool slightly. Serve warm on any salad.

**Tip:** Pink pepper is still spicy, but has a slightly sweet, fruity aroma. I tried these croutons with black pepper, but there is something about the buttery toasted bread cubes tossed with pink pepper and crunchy salt that really seems to bring out the flavors so much more intensely. In fact, when I was testing these croutons, Ryan was eating them hot, straight from the pan!

## INGREDIENTS & PREP

### LEMON VINAIGRETTE

**Lemon Zest** – 2 teaspoons

**Lemon Juice** – ½ cup, freshly squeezed

**Honey** – 4 teaspoons

**Dijon Mustard** – 1½ teaspoons

**Olive Oil** – ½ cup

**Sea Salt** – 1 teaspoon

**Black Pepper** – 1 teaspoon, freshly cracked

—

*Makes ²⁄₃ cup*

### BRIOCHE CROUTONS

**Butter** – 3 tablespoons, unsalted, French recommended

**Brioche** – 4 slices, ¾-inch diced (about 3 cups)

**Fleur de Sel** – ¾ teaspoon

**Pink Pepper** – 1 teaspoon, freshly cracked

# Creamy Roasted Potatoes

## A PERFECT HEARTY PAIRING FOR ANY OMELETTE

## DIRECTIONS

① Preheat the oven to 400 degrees F.

② Place the cut potatoes onto a half sheet pan. Toss with olive oil, thyme, garlic, salt, and pepper. Arrange them in a single layer.

③ Roast for 40 – 45 minutes, in the center of the oven, until the edges are crisp and browned, tossing once during the cooking process.

④ Serve immediately.

Idea: This is the most basic recipe for roasting the smaller varieties of potatoes. While these are completely delicious and flavorful as they are, experiment with different garnishes: Fresh parsley, smoked paprika, freshly grated Parmesan cheese, or truffle salt. These are perfect for serving alongside any of my French omelettes.

## INGREDIENTS & PREP

Small Potatoes – 2 pounds, cut in half lengthwise, baby Yukon Gold variety

Olive Oil – 5 tablespoons

Thyme – 7 sprigs, fresh

Garlic – 6 cloves, peeled and smashed

Sea Salt – 1 teaspoon

Black Pepper – 1 teaspoon, freshly cracked

—

*Serves 4*

## NOTES

_____

_____

_____

_____

_____

_____

_____

# Roasted Red Onions *with* Tarragon

## A TOUCH OF ANISE MAKES THESE ONIONS SOIRÉE-READY

## DIRECTIONS

① Preheat the oven to 400 degrees F.

② Place the tarragon, onions, salt, and pepper onto a half sheet pan. Drizzle with olive oil and toss together, being careful not to break up the individual wedges of onions.

③ Roast, in the center of the oven, for 22 – 24 minutes until the onions are tender. Serve hot.

**Tip**: In addition to serving these fragrant onions as a side dish, they are also wonderful as part of a cheese board or tossed in a simple salad dressed with my *French Bistro Vinaigrette* (page 115).

## INGREDIENTS & PREP

**Tarragon** – 10 sprigs, fresh

**Red Onions** – 3 large, peeled and ends trimmed, each cut into 8 wedges (cut through the root end to keep the wedges intact)

**Sea Salt** – 1 teaspoon

**Black Pepper** – 1 teaspoon, freshly cracked

**Olive Oil** – 7 tablespoons, divided

—

*Serves 4*

## NOTES

_____

_____

_____

_____

_____

_____

_____

# Vinaigrette Vert

IMAGINE THE GREEN GODDESS DRESSING WEARING A BERET

## DIRECTIONS

① In the bowl of a food processor fitted with a steel blade, add all of the ingredients, reserving the olive oil.

② Pulse a few times to combine the crème fraîche and fresh herbs.

③ With the motor running, slowly pour the olive oil down the feed tube.

④ Transfer the dressing to a serving bowl and serve alongside a green salad.

**Tip:** You can also serve this vinaigrette as a dip for a vegetable crudité, use as a sauce on grilled or roasted vegetables and as a spread on tartines and sandwiches.

## INGREDIENTS & PREP

Crème Fraîche - ½ cup

Sherry Vinegar - 1 teaspoon

Dill - ½ cup, fresh, roughly chopped

Tarragon - ¼ cup, fresh, roughly chopped

Basil - ¼ cup, fresh, roughly chopped

Chives - 3 tablespoons, fresh, roughly chopped

Mint - 1 tablespoon, fresh, roughly chopped

Parsley - 1 cup, fresh, roughly chopped, Italian flat-leaf variety

Garlic - 2 cloves, roughly chopped

Lemon Juice - 3 tablespoons, freshly squeezed

Black Pepper - ½ teaspoon, freshly cracked

Fleur de Sel - ½ teaspoon

Olive Oil - ½ cup

—

*Makes 1 cup*

## NOTES

# White Wine Buttered Vegetables

## THE MOST ELEGANT (AND VERSATILE!) 10-MINUTE SIDE DISH

### DIRECTIONS

① In a large heavy-bottomed pan with a tight-fitting lid set over medium heat, add the wine and butter.

② Once hot, add the remaining ingredients, reserving the peas, and stir to coat the vegetables in the wine and butter. Cover and allow to steam for 4 – 6 minutes, shaking the pan every couple of minutes, until the vegetables are tender but not soft.

③ Lastly, remove the pan from the heat, add the peas, cover and allow to sit for 1 minute. Garnish with more salt and pepper and serve hot.

**Tip**: You can serve these buttery, tender vegetables right from the pan tableside or transfer them to a large platter, making sure to spoon over all of the liquid from the pan.

**Serving Idea**: Depending on which omelette you are serving alongside these fabulous vegetables, a handful of fresh herbs, or even a combination of herbs, is a welcomed addition. Herbs like tarragon, Italian flat-leaf parsley, dill, or even mint, are just a few options to add to this earthy side dish.

### INGREDIENTS & PREP

**White Wine** – ½ cup, dry French Chardonnay recommended

**Butter** – 6 tablespoons, unsalted, at room temperature, French recommended

**Frozen Artichoke Hearts** – 12 ounces, defrosted

**Leeks** – 2 cups, thinly sliced, white and light green parts, cleaned of all sand

**French Green Beans** – 6 ounces, ends trimmed

**Lemon** – 1 large, zested

**Sea Salt** – 2 teaspoons

**Black Pepper** – 1 teaspoon, freshly cracked

**Frozen Peas** – 10 ounces, defrosted

—

*Serves 4*

# Heirloom Tomato & Herb Salad
## YOUR LOCAL FARM STAND ON A PLATE

### DIRECTIONS

① Cut the large tomatoes in thick slices, the medium ones into wedges, and the smaller ones in half—you can even leave a few smaller ones whole.

② Choose a large platter or shallow serving bowl and arrange the tomatoes so you have varying sizes and colors mixed together and drizzle with olive oil. Sprinkle with fleur de sel and black pepper.

③ Next, scatter all of the fresh herbs onto the tomatoes. Drizzle with more olive oil and garnish with more fleur de sel and black pepper.

**Tip:** Whether you buy your tomatoes from the farmers market, farm stand, or grocery store, leave them in a warm, sunny window for at least 4 hours before serving. The sun will warm them up and help release the natural sugars and add even more flavor!

### INGREDIENTS & PREP

**Heirloom Tomatoes** - 3 pounds, varying sizes and colors, stem-end cored out of larger tomatoes

**Olive Oil** - ½ cup, plus more for serving

**Fleur de Sel** - 1½ teaspoons, plus more for garnish

**Black Pepper** - 1½ teaspoons, freshly cracked, plus more for garnish

**Basil** - ½ cup, whole leaves, fresh

**Parsley** - ½ cup, whole leaves, fresh, Italian flat-leaf variety

**Mint** - ½ cup, whole leaves, fresh

**Dill** - ½ cup, whole fronds, fresh

**Chives** - ½ cup, fresh, trimmed to 1½-inch lengths

**Tarragon** - ½ cup, whole leaves, fresh

*Serves 4*

### NOTES

_____
_____
_____
_____
_____
_____
_____

# French Bistro Vinaigrette
## A PARIS STAPLE, REIMAGINED

### DIRECTIONS

① Place all of the ingredients into a jar with a tight-fitting lid. Shake vigorously for about 60 seconds.

② Refrigerate for at least 30 minutes before dressing a salad.

Tip: This is, by far, my favorite vinaigrette and one that I keep constantly on hand. It can be prepared up to 7 days in advance and stored in the same jar in which it was made. Just remember to make sure you are using fresh egg yolks in order for it to maintain its shelf life.

### INGREDIENTS & PREP

Egg Yolk – 1 extra-large, at room temperature

Sea Salt – ½ teaspoon

Black Pepper – ½ teaspoon, freshly cracked

Champagne Vinegar – 2 tablespoons

Crème Fraîche – 1 tablespoon

Dijon Mustard – 2 teaspoons

Garlic – 1 clove, crushed (using a garlic press)

Vegetable Oil – 7 tablespoons

Olive Oil – 1 tablespoon

—

*Makes 1¼ cups*

### NOTES

# French Carrot Salad

## A PARISIAN TAKE ON AN AMERICAN DELI CLASSIC

## DIRECTIONS

*SALAD*

① In a large bowl, add the carrots, whole parsley leaves, and chives. Set aside.

*VINAIGRETTE & ASSEMBLY*

② Place all of the ingredients into a jar with a tight-fitting lid. Shake vigorously for about 60 seconds.

③ Pour the vinaigrette over the carrot mixture and toss.

④ Transfer the salad to a serving bowl or platter, garnish with more salt and pepper, and serve at room temperature.

**Tip**: You can make the vinaigrette up to 3 days in advance and store in it the refrigerator in the same jar in which it was made.

**Trick**: Don't skip the step of shredding the carrots yourself. I like to use top carrots (carrots that still have the greens attached) because these tend to be the freshest available in the grocery store and have the best flavor. While it may be appealing to save a few extra minutes and use pre-shredded carrots, who knows how long they have been in that bag! If you can find rainbow or tri-colored carrots, these will add a big color boost to this already beautiful and earthy salad.

## INGREDIENTS & PREP

*SALAD*

**Carrots** – 1 pound, peeled and finely shredded

**Parsley** – 1 cup, whole leaves, fresh, Italian flat-leaf variety

**Chives** – $\frac{1}{3}$ cup, fresh, finely minced

—

*Serves 6*

*VINAIGRETTE*

**Olive Oil** – 3 tablespoons

**Honey** – 1 teaspoon

**Dijon Mustard** – 1½ teaspoons

**Crème Fraîche** – 1 tablespoon

**Lemon Juice** – 2 tablespoons, freshly squeezed

**Fleur de Sel** – ½ teaspoon

**Black Pepper** – ½ teaspoon, freshly cracked

# Provençal Vegetable Tian

## A QUINTESSENTIAL FRENCH COUNTRY RECIPE

### DIRECTIONS

① Preheat the oven to 400 degrees F. Line a half sheet pan with parchment paper. Set aside.

② Slice the tomatoes, zucchini, and eggplant between ⅛-inch to ¼-inch thick (a mandolin makes quick work of this step—but a sharp knife will work perfectly fine, too) and organize them into piles.

③ Pour 3 tablespoons of olive oil into a 1½ – 2 quart straight-sided oven-safe baking dish. Scatter half of the garlic, 3 sprigs of rosemary, and 5 sprigs of thyme in the bottom of the dish.

④ Next, layer the vegetables alternately in the dish until you have used up all of the vegetables. Don't be afraid to pack them tightly. Tuck the remaining garlic slices in between the layers of vegetables.

⑤ Scatter the remaining sprigs of fresh herbs across the top, drizzle evenly with 7 tablespoons of olive oil and sprinkle with salt and pepper. Place the baking dish onto the parchment-lined half sheet pan.

⑥ Bake, in the center of the oven, for 70 – 80 minutes, until the vegetables are velvety tender. Remove the tian from the oven, scatter bits of butter over the top, and allow it to cool for 5 minutes. Serve hot or room temperature.

### INGREDIENTS & PREP

**Tomatoes** – 1 pound, vine-ripened recommended, stem-end cored out

**Zucchini** – 1 pound, green and yellow, ends trimmed

**Graffiti Eggplant** – ½ pound, ends trimmed

**Olive Oil** – 10 tablespoons

**Garlic** – 4 cloves, thinly sliced

**Rosemary** – 6 sprigs, fresh

**Thyme** – 10 sprigs, fresh

**Sea Salt** – 1 teaspoon

**Black Pepper** – 1 teaspoon, freshly cracked

**Butter** – 2 teaspoons, unsalted, at room temperature, French recommended

—

*Serves 4*

Tip: Not only is this tian a perfect side dish, all of the oil that collects in the bottom of the baking dish has the most amazing flavor from the vegetables, herbs, and garlic. Have an extra baguette (or two!) on hand for dipping!

# Flourless Chocolate & Cognac Cake

## A CLOUD-LIKE CHOCOLATE DECADENCE, IN JUST 30 MINUTES

### DIRECTIONS

① Preheat oven to 350 degrees F. Butter an 8-inch round cake pan. Line the bottom of the pan with a piece of parchment paper. Butter the top of the parchment paper. Lightly dust the entire pan with cocoa powder. Set aside.

② In a medium heat-proof bowl set over a pan of barely simmering water, melt the chopped chocolate, butter, honey, cream, and salt, stirring occasionally until the mixture is completely smooth. Allow the chocolate to cool for 10 minutes.

③ Next, add the cocoa powder, cinnamon, sugar, vanilla, and 1 tablespoon of cognac. Stir to combine. Whisk in the eggs one at a time. Using a spatula, scrape down the sides and bottom of the bowl, making sure everything is well-mixed.

④ Pour the batter into the prepared pan and bake, in the center of the oven, for 24 – 27 minutes, or until the top is set. The cake will still be a bit wobbly.

### INGREDIENTS & PREP

**Butter** - 8 tablespoons, unsalted, French recommended, plus more for preparing pan

**Cocoa Powder** - ½ cup, unsweetened, Pernigotti recommended, plus more for preparing pan

**Dark Chocolate** - 5 ounces, 72% cocoa, roughly chopped

**Honey** - 2 tablespoons

**Heavy Cream** - 3 tablespoons

**Sea Salt** - ¼ teaspoon

**Cinnamon** - ¼ teaspoon

**Dark Brown Sugar** - ¾ cup, lightly packed

**Vanilla** - 1 teaspoon, pure extract

**Cognac** - 3 tablespoons, divided, Remy Martin 1739 recommended

**Eggs** - 5 extra-large, at room temperature

**Crème Fraîche** - for serving, at room temperature

—

*Serves 4, with enough left over for another night's indulgence!*

⑤ Remove the pan from the oven and very slowly drizzle over the remaining 2 tablespoons of cognac, allowing it to fully absorb into the top and down the sides of the hot cake.

⑥ Allow the cake to cool in the pan for 10 minutes. Carefully remove the cake from the pan and allow to finish cooling on a cooling rack. Serve with a bowl of crème fraîche on the side.

# Assiette *de* Fromage

## A MUST-SERVE FOR ANY FRENCH MEAL

**Presentation**—a cheese plate is a must when entertaining French-style! Cheese is presented in smaller amounts and seen as something to nibble on as you and your guests bridge the time between the main course and the dessert. And sometimes cheese takes the place of dessert. A single variety is served, and sometimes an assortment depending on the number of guests at your soirée. It is presented elegantly on a wooden board or a dinner plate. You can also make individual servings on salad or dessert plates—this is especially lovely as it really makes an impression of thoughtfulness. I let the cheese sit at room temperature for at least 30 minutes before serving (never serve cheese straight from the refrigerator). This helps to showcase the natural texture and flavor. Whichever way you choose, your presentation should be simple and restrained—and never gluttonous!

**Accompaniments**—you can create a beautiful *assiette* with things like fresh and dried fruits, slices of baguette, hearty crackers, cornichons, preserves, and fresh herbs, tucked into one another—in small quantities. When available, I add edible flowers from the grocery store for color, texture, and taste—guests are always surprised and delighted by culinary blooms. Less is more when it comes to any selection of accompaniments.

**Cheese**—many grocery stores now carry a fabulous assortment of the most common and recognizable types of French cheeses. If you have a specialty cheese shop in your town, ask them to recommend a few types to pair with your menu—in some cases they will even place special orders. But if you are shopping at your local grocery store, these are the five types of French cheese most readily found:

**Comté** - a hard, unpasteurized cow's milk cheese with a slightly nutty flavor (Gruyère is similar in flavor and a perfect substitute)

**Roquefort** - a creamy, sheep's milk cheese with a pungent flavor (think of it as a more flavorful blue cheese similar to the texture of Gorgonzola)

**Camembert** - a soft-ripening, cow's milk cheese with an edible white rind and an earthy, grassy and even mushroom-y flavor (with a soft and creamy texture)

**Chèvre** - a goat's milk cheese with a tangy kick (pictured to the left drizzled with olive oil, pink pepper, fleur de sel, and fresh thyme leaves)

**Mimolette** - a hard cheese with a sweet and subtle caramel flavor (it has a fudgy texture and electric-orange color)

# Elderflower Cosmo

## A SWEET AND FLORAL-INFUSED FRENCH-KISSED COCKTAIL

### DIRECTIONS

1. Fill a large cocktail shaker with ice. Add all of the ingredients, reserving the mint, and shake for 60 seconds.

2. Strain the cocktail into a martini glass, garnish with a sprig of mint, and serve immediately.

**Tip:** While the recipe makes one good-sized cocktail per person, sometimes the "I'll have one more" happens, so why not be prepared? You can double the recipe, fill a glass pitcher with the cocktail ingredients, reserving the mint, and let it sit in the refrigerator. When a guest needs a cocktail, simply fill a cocktail shaker with ice, then fill the shaker with *Cosmo* mix, shake, strain, garnish, and serve. Et voilà!

### INGREDIENTS & PREP

**Vodka** – 1 cup, Grey Goose recommended

**Elderflower Liqueur** – ½ cup, St-Germain recommended

**Cranberry Juice** – ½ cup

**Lemon Juice** – ¼ cup, freshly squeezed

**Mint** – for garnish, fresh

—

*Serves 4*

### NOTES

_____

_____

_____

_____

_____

_____

# Recipe Index

*"Thoughtful details versus grand gestures, are what people will always remember."*

—*Marc J. Sievers*

# Recipe Index

OMELETTES

# Recipe Index
## OMELETTES

# Recipe Index
COMPONENTS

$\underline{\mathbf{m}}$

Visit *MarcSievers.com* for more

CPSIA information can be obtained
at www.ICGtesting.com
Printed in the USA
BVRC090026071221
623077BV00055B/712